To:_____

From:_____

MOTHERS & SONS
Why Sons Always Need Their Mothers

Written by Dana Bottenfield

new seasons®

A SON NEEDS A MOTHER...

...to teach him when to lead and when to follow.

A SON NEEDS A MOTHER...

...to be there for his family.

A SON NEEDS A MOTHER...

...to keep traditions alive.

...to help him find his courage.

A SON NEEDS A MOTHER...

...to encourage brotherly love.

A SON NEEDS A MOTHER...

...to play with when it snows.

A SON NEEDS A MOTHER...

...to keep him close.

A SON NEEDS A MOTHER...

...to recognize accomplishments big and small.

A son needs a mother...

...to give him a push to get himself started.

...to give him the tools to be independent.

...to show him how to dance.

A SON NEEDS A MOTHER...

...to help him find balance in his life.

A SON NEEDS A MOTHER...

...to show him both patience and persistence.

A SON NEEDS A MOTHER...

...to make things all better.

A SON NEEDS A MOTHER...

...to retell his most triumphant moments.

A SON NEEDS A MOTHER...

...to show him how to treat a friend.

A SON NEEDS A MOTHER...

...to find what's special in each of us.

A SON NEEDS A MOTHER...

...to show him how to take
care of the world around him.

⌒◉⌒

A SON NEEDS A MOTHER...

…to show him that you should
always have a sense of humor.

A SON NEEDS A MOTHER...

...to teach him how to drive.

A SON NEEDS A MOTHER...

...to set boundaries in his life.

A SON NEEDS A MOTHER...

...to provide an honest and fair opinion.

A SON NEEDS A MOTHER...

...to help him stay true to himself.

A SON NEEDS A MOTHER...

...to show him how to be a straight-shooter.

A SON NEEDS A MOTHER...

...to help him celebrate his birthday.

A SON NEEDS A MOTHER...

…to hold him up until he can support himself.

A SON NEEDS A MOTHER...

...to give him safety and warmth.

A SON NEEDS A MOTHER...

...to let him rock out.

A SON NEEDS A MOTHER...

...to show him how to spread his wings.

A SON NEEDS A MOTHER...

...to encourage his creativity.

A SON NEEDS A MOTHER...

...to teach him about the world around him.

A son needs a mother...

...to welcome his new family.

A son needs a mother...

...to teach him life's most important skills.

A SON NEEDS A MOTHER...

...to teach him street smarts.

A SON NEEDS A MOTHER...

...to walk him through his first steps.

A SON NEEDS A MOTHER...

...to help him make wishes for the future.